WHAT *IS* BAPTISM?

The Crucial Questions Series
By R. C. Sproul

CRUCIAL
QUESTIONS
No. 11

WHAT *IS* BAPTISM?

R.C. SPROUL

ℝ *Reformation Trust*   A DIVISION OF LIGONIER MINISTRIES, ORLANDO, FL

What Is Baptism?

© 2011 by R.C. Sproul

Published by Reformation Trust Publishing
a division of Ligonier Ministries
421 Ligonier Court, Sanford, FL 32771
Ligonier.org   ReformationTrust.com

Printed in North Mankato, MN
Corporate Graphics
November 2012
First edition, second printing

Cover design: Gearbox Studios
Interior design and typeset: Katherine Lloyd, The DESK

All Scripture quotations are from *The Holy Bible, English Standard Version*®, copyright © 2001 by Crossway Bibles, a publishing ministry of Good News Publishers. Used by permission. All rights reserved.

Library of Congress Cataloging-in-Publication Data

Sproul, R. C. (Robert Charles), 1939-
  What is baptism? / R.C. Sproul.
    p. cm.
  Includes bibliographical references.
  ISBN 978-1-56769-260-0
1. Baptism--Reformed Church. 2. Reformed Church--Doctrines. I. Title.
BX9427.5.B36.S67 2011
234'.161--dc23

2011020970

Contents

Chapter One

BAPTISM AND SALVATION

One of the most stirring descriptions of the church is found in Ephesians 4:4–6, where we read: "There is one body and one Spirit—just as you were called to the one hope that belongs to your call—one Lord, one faith, one baptism, one God and Father of all, who is over all and through all and in all." The church is one body filled with one Spirit and united around one hope, worshiping one Lord and one God in one faith. And, we are told, there is one baptism.

Thanks to this passage and numerous other biblical affirmations, the sacrament of baptism has occupied a central role in the church throughout its history and is an important aspect of Christian worship. Yet we find that a great deal of controversy surrounds the subject of baptism. It seems there are questions over just about every aspect of the sacrament: the origin or institution of baptism; the meaning of baptism; the administration of baptism (Who is permitted and authorized to baptize people?); the formula for baptism (Is baptism to be administered only in the name of Jesus or in the names of all three persons of the Trinity?); the mode of baptism (Is baptism to be by sprinkling, pouring, dipping, or immersion?); and the proper recipients of baptism (Is it restricted to adults who have made credible professions of faith or may infants be baptized as well?). Another major controversy has to do with the efficacy of the sacrament (What does baptism actually accomplish in the lives of those who receive it?).

Given that we have one Lord, one faith, and one baptism, we might think that there would be fewer questions surrounding this sacrament. It is tragic that Christians are so sharply divided about these issues. And yet, the divisions and the controversies show that Christians recognize that baptism is a serious matter. After all, no one can read the New Testament, even in a cursory manner, and not clearly see that baptism is a very important element of the Christian faith. So Christians who take their faith seriously also take baptism seriously, and they want to get it right. They care enough about baptism to debate areas of uncertainty.

Without a doubt, the greatest controversy over baptism has centered on its role in salvation. Must a person be baptized to experience the new birth? This question has been an enormous point of contention in the history of the church, so I want to address it in this opening chapter.

FAITH VS. BAPTISM

The Roman Catholic Church sees the sacrament of baptism as the instrumental cause of justification. What does Rome mean by that? To help answer that question, I want us to look back to the ancient Greek philosopher Aristotle, who articulated the idea of instrumental causality.

Aristotle identified various types of causes. His favorite

illustration of the various causes involved a statue. He said a statue has several causes, several things that must be present for the image to take shape. First, he said, there has to be a *material cause*, which he defined as the material from which the statue is made. It could be a block of stone, a chunk of wood, or some other substance. He then identified the *efficient cause*, a person who changes the shape of the material and refashions it. For a statue, the efficient cause is the sculptor. Next there is the *formal cause*, a plan, idea, or blueprint that directs the alteration of the material. There is also a *final cause*, which is the reason for the statue. Finally, Aristotle identified the *instrumental cause*, which is the tool or means by which the change in the material is wrought. In sculpting his *Pieta*, Michelangelo could not just command the marble to take the shape he desired. He needed a chisel and a hammer. Those were the instruments by which the change in the marble took place.

As Protestants, we say that justification is by faith alone. That little word *by* is critical to our understanding of how justification takes place. It does not mean that faith is meritorious and obligates God to save us. Rather, the word *by* indicates grammatically what we call the instrumental dative, which describes the means by which a thing comes to pass.

So, to use Aristotle's categories, faith is the instrumental cause of justification, according to the Protestant view.

By contrast, the Roman Catholic Church says the instrumental cause of justification is baptism. Rome proclaims that a person is justified when he or she is baptized by a priest. At baptism, the person receives an infusion, an inpouring, of grace in the soul. This grace is sometimes called the grace of the righteousness of Christ or the grace of justification. When it is infused into the soul of the person who is being baptized, that person enters a state of grace.

A SECOND PLANK OF JUSTIFICATION

In the Roman Catholic view, it is necessary for the person who is baptized to cooperate with infused grace to stay in a state of grace, because, according to Rome, people can lose their justification. If a person commits a very serious sin, the grace of justification is killed. Thus, the Roman Catholic Church calls such sins "mortal sins."

Since saving grace is infused into a person at baptism, it would seem that if a baptized person commits a mortal sin, thus wiping out the grace of justification in his or her soul, in order to be justified again, the person would have to be baptized again. But the Roman Catholic Church does not rebaptize people who commit mortal sins; it teaches that even though justification is lost by mortal sin, there is a *character indelibilis*, an indelible mark that is placed on the soul of everyone who is baptized.

Thus, restoration to justification in the event of mortal sin is through another sacrament, penance, which the Roman Catholic Church describes as the second plank of justification for those who have made shipwreck of their souls (the sacrament of penance was what provoked the controversy that led to the Protestant Reformation in the sixteenth century). So the first instrumental cause of justification is the sacrament of baptism. If you lose your justification, the next time the instrumental cause is the sacrament of penance. In short, according to Rome, sacraments are the instruments by which salvation is communicated.

"FROM THE WORKING OF THE WORK"

As part of its argument for the efficacy of the sacraments, the Roman Catholic Church states that they function *ex opere operato*, which means literally, "From the working of the work." When the Protestant Reformers began to question

Rome's teachings, they asserted that *ex opere operato* must mean that anyone who is baptized automatically is justified. Roman Catholic authorities replied that justification is not automatic, for the infusion of grace that occurs at baptism does not lead to justification if the recipient hinders it with unbelief. Incidentally, this means that those who are baptized as infants are certainly justified because they are not capable of resisting the infusion of grace.

Against the *ex opere operato* principle of Rome, the Reformers argued that the benefits signified by baptism are not received apart from faith. When God gives the sign of baptism to a person, He gives a promise of all of the benefits that He will bestow on all who believe. Therefore, a person can be baptized and yet never come to faith and never experience all of the benefits that we have enumerated. So classical Reformed theology repudiates the idea of any kind of automatic efficacy of baptism.

Does that mean that baptism is simply an empty sign? Why do it if it does not accomplish anything? We do it first because Christ commanded it, but also because it conveys the sign of the promise of God of salvation by faith and all of the benefits that flow from that. When a person is baptized and comes to faith, if he later worries about the loss of his salvation, he can recall his baptism—not because the baptism guarantees his salvation, but because it reminds him of the unfailing promise of God to preserve all those who are engrafted into Christ. As we will see, when Abraham asked how he could be sure that God would fulfill His promise to give Abraham the land of Canaan, God went through a covenant ceremony. In other words, God took an oath. He made a covenant promise, saying, in essence, "Abraham, may I be destroyed if I do not keep my promise to you."

God does not promise any of the benefits of salvation to unbelievers. The promise is only to those who believe, and the promise is absolutely sure for them. Therefore, baptism is infinitely valuable.

Baptism, then, is not necessary for salvation. We have only to consider the example of the thief on the cross; he was not baptized, yet Jesus promised that he would be in paradise that day. Some who believe are physically hindered from being baptized, and some people refrain because they believe it's not necessary. I still believe they will be in heaven if they have truly trusted Christ alone for their salvation.

The debate over the place of baptism in the salvation of

sinners is but one of the controversies that have attended this sacrament through the centuries. My goal in this booklet is to touch on some of these disputes. I will not go into detail, but I hope to provide an overview and introduction to some of the key issues that surround this sacrament.

Chapter Two

JOHN'S BAPTISM AND JESUS' BAPTISM

We first encounter baptism in the Scriptures when John the Baptist arrives on the scene. John ministered before Jesus commissioned His disciples to baptize (Matt. 28:19) or said anything at all about baptism. We are given bits of information about John's ministry in all four gospel accounts, but Luke provides perhaps the most extensive look at his life and work. We read there:

In the fifteenth year of the reign of Tiberius Caesar, Pontius Pilate being governor of Judea, and Herod being tetrarch of Galilee, and his brother Philip tetrarch of the region of Ituraea and Trachonitis, and Lysanias tetrarch of Abilene, during the high priesthood of Annas and Caiaphas, the word of God came to John the son of Zechariah in the wilderness. And he went into all the region around the Jordan, proclaiming a baptism of repentance for the forgiveness of sins. As it is written in the book of the words of Isaiah the prophet, "The voice of one crying in the wilderness: 'Prepare the way of the Lord, make his paths straight. Every valley shall be filled, and every mountain and hill shall be made low, and the crooked shall become straight, and the rough places shall become level ways, and all flesh shall see the salvation of God.'" (3:1–6)

Clearly the New Testament apostles understood the advent of John the Baptist in the context of Isaiah's prophecy of one who would come as the herald of the Messiah, one whose chief responsibility in God's plan of redemption would be to prepare the way for the coming of the Lord.

They were also well aware of a prophecy in the book of the prophet Malachi. In the last chapter of his book—indeed, in the last paragraph of his book—Malachi talked about the coming "day of the LORD," which would not take place until Elijah the prophet reappeared (Mal. 4:5). So, for four hundred years after Malachi, the Jewish people looked for the return of the prophet Elijah, who had been taken to heaven hundreds of years before (2 Kings 2:11). At every celebration of the Passover, an empty chair was placed at the table in commemoration of Elijah, should he come and be a guest that night.

Therefore, it is not surprising that when John began to attract attention, "the Jews sent priests and Levites from Jerusalem to ask him, 'Who are you?' He confessed, and did not deny, but confessed, 'I am not the Christ.' And they asked him, 'What then? Are you Elijah?' He said, 'I am not'" (John 1:19–21a). When John put to rest any thoughts that he might be the Messiah, the authorities next guessed that he was Elijah. But John denied that, too.

This denial is rather mysterious, for an angel had said John would "go before [the Lord] in the spirit and power of Elijah" (Luke 1:17), and Jesus later said, "If you are willing to accept it, [John] is Elijah who is to come," and, "'I tell you that Elijah has already come, and they did not recognize him, but did to him whatever they pleased.'... Then the disciples understood that he was speaking to them of John the Baptist" (Matt. 11:14; 17:12–13). However, the way in which Jesus qualified those comments, and the angel's statement that John would be "in the spirit and power of Elijah," indicate that John was not the actual Elijah. However, there was a continuity between them, such that the ministry of Elijah was reintroduced in the person of John the Baptist.

THE END OF THE SILENCE?

Try to imagine that you are a first-century Jew. Suddenly, it seems everyone is talking about the appearance of a man of God coming from the wilderness, the desert, which was the traditional meeting place between God and His prophets in the Old Testament. In the desert, the prophet would receive his anointing; there he would be given the Word of God and commissioned to proclaim it in Israel. People soon began to wonder whether John was a prophet.

This question was full of significance because there had been a long period of prophetic silence. In the accounts of the Old Testament, it seems as if there's a prophet behind every bush. That was an era when prophecy was very important to the life of the Israelites, and Elijah stood at the head of the list of the prophets. But then, suddenly, the prophetic Word of God had ceased in the land. Malachi had been the last prophet in Israel. There had been no word from God for four hundred years. The people of Israel had been waiting for what seemed an eternity for God to speak again. Thus, hope quickly soared that John was bringing the long-awaited word from God.

I have a trick question I like to pose to my students: "Who was the greatest prophet in the Old Testament?" Some say Elijah; some say Isaiah; others insist on Jeremiah. Finally I say, "No, the greatest prophet in the Old Testament was John the Baptist." We sometimes forget that while we read about John the Baptist in the New Testament, he lived before Jesus inaugurated the new covenant in the upper room on the night of His betrayal. So the economy of the old covenant extended from the beginning in the garden of Eden to the time of the Last Supper. Thus, John the Baptist belonged to the period of the Old Testament, and Jesus said of him, "Among those born of women there has arisen no one greater than John the Baptist" (Matt. 11:11).

"THE KINGDOM OF GOD IS AT HAND"

While John was the greatest Old Testament prophet, it was his task to announce the end of the period of Old Testament redemptive history, for the kingdom of God was about to break through. In the Old Testament, the arrival of the kingdom of God was an ambiguous future event. But John began his message with a radical note of urgency. He cried out, "Repent, for the kingdom of God is at hand" (Matt. 3:2). He was saying that the kingdom of God was not in the distant future, it was about to arrive.

John used two metaphors to illustrate the urgency of the hour. First, he said, "Even now the axe is laid at the root of the trees" (Matt. 3:10a). It wasn't as if the woodsman had just gone out into the forest and started to chip away at the bark of a tree, but he still had to swing his ax another thousand times before he could bring it down. Rather, the woodsman had already cut down to the very heart and core of the tree. John was saying that with one more blow from the ax, the tree would come down.

Second, John said, "His winnowing fork is in his hand, and he will clear his threshing floor and gather his wheat into the barn, but the chaff he will burn with unquenchable fire" (Matt. 3:12). The winnowing fork was a tool used by grain farmers to separate the wheat from the chaff. After the grain was threshed, that is, the seeds were separated from the husks, the farmer would use a large fork to toss piles of seed into the air so that the wind would blow away the lighter chaff, the final small pieces of the husks. The chaff would blow away, but the heavier seeds would fall back into the pile. John was saying that the farmer was not just thinking about separating the wheat from the chaff, nor was he walking to the barn to get his winnowing fork. Instead, the farmer's winnowing fork was in his hand and he was about to begin the final step in the processing of his harvest. The moment of separation, the crisis moment that would divide the good wheat from the useless and undesirable chaff, was about to happen. John was saying, "Israel, your King is about to come, the Messiah is at hand, and you're not ready."

THE SCANDAL OF BAPTISM

What did the people need to do to be ready for the Messiah's arrival? John told them plainly: they needed to repent of their sins and be baptized.

In the minds of the theologians and rulers of the day, John's call for the Jewish people to present themselves at the Jordan River to be baptized was scandalous. Why? When a Gentile converted to Judaism, he had to embrace the tenets and doctrines of Judaism, and he had to be circumcised. In addition, he had to undergo a ritual that had developed during the intertestamental period, a ceremonial bath of purification known as "proselyte baptism." This rite of purification was administered to Gentile converts because the Jews considered the Gentiles to be ceremonially unclean. The Jews, by contrast, were considered to be clean, so they were not required to undergo any sort of cleansing rite. But when John called them to be baptized, the Pharisees were outraged by his implication that the Jews were unclean. They could not see that God was imposing a new requirement on His people because a new moment in redemptive history was at hand—the arrival of the Messiah—and even the Jews needed remission of their sins.

One day, as John was baptizing at the Jordan River, he saw Jesus approaching. He cried out, "Behold, the Lamb of God, who takes away the sin of the world!" (John 1:29b). Then Jesus came to John and asked to be baptized. John was stunned. Matthew tells us that "John would have prevented him, saying, 'I need to be baptized by you, and do you come to me?'" (3:14). He knew Jesus was sinless and therefore had no need of a cleansing ritual. But Jesus said, "Let it be so now, for thus it is fitting for us to fulfill all righteousness" (v. 15). As the Messiah, Jesus had to submit Himself to the entire law of God. His vocation was not simply to die for the sins of His people, He also had to obey the law perfectly to achieve the righteousness that would be imputed to those people. Every requirement imposed on Israel was imposed on Israel's Messiah—including the command to be baptized, which command was delivered by John the Baptist, a prophet of God. So Jesus was baptized.

As we consider John's baptism, however, it is vital that we understand that it is not equivalent to New Testament baptism. There are many points of similarity, but the two are not the same. New Testament baptism goes beyond what was involved in and signified by John's baptism. His baptism was a preparatory rite for the Jewish people as they awaited the coming Messiah, so its meaning was rooted and grounded in the Old Testament. It served as a bridge to the New Testament sacrament of baptism. Later, Jesus commanded something with a deeper, greater significance.

BAPTISM COMMANDED

At the end of Matthew's gospel, we find a climactic communication between Jesus and His disciples. Matthew writes:

> Now the eleven disciples went to Galilee, to the mountain to which Jesus had directed them. And when they saw him they worshiped him, but some doubted. And Jesus came and said to them, "All authority in heaven and on earth has been given to me. Go therefore and make disciples of all nations, baptizing them in the name of the Father and of the Son and of the Holy Spirit, teaching them to observe all that I have commanded you. And behold, I am with you always, to the end of the age." (28:16–20)

It is significant, I think, that Jesus prefaced this mandate by telling His disciples, "All authority in heaven and on earth has been given to me." In all of His teaching until the time of His crucifixion, Jesus never commanded baptism. But He did so here. Having risen from the grave, He had the authority, because of His finished work, to create a new sign for the new covenant, and He did just that in commanding baptism.

In the previous chapter, I asserted that baptism is not necessary for salvation. However, if you were to ask me, "Is baptism necessary for the Christian?" I would say, "Absolutely." It is not necessary for salvation, but it is necessary for obedience, because Christ, with no ambiguity, commanded that all of those who belong to Him, who are part of the new covenant family, and who receive the benefits of His salvation are to be baptized in the Trinitarian formula.

Chapter Three

The Sign of the Covenant

I don't know when it became a custom for American Christians to ask conference speakers to sign their Bibles, but I get that request frequently when I speak. In many instances, the people asking me to sign their Bibles will request that I write my "life verse." This request took me by surprise when I first began to encounter it. I did not have a life verse; I suppose I wanted to have the whole counsel of God as a banner over my life. But since people wanted a verse, I began to write down this verse or that. The one I have given most frequently is Genesis 15:17, which says, "When the sun had gone down and it was dark, behold, a smoking fire pot and a flaming torch passed between these pieces."

You may be scratching your head at this moment as you ponder why I would choose to share this verse. Let me assure you, you are not alone. When I write Genesis 15:17 in people's Bibles, invariably, before the conference ends, someone comes up to me and asks, "Did you mean to write Genesis 15:17 in my Bible?" When I assure the person that I did, he or she often says, "That verse doesn't make sense to me."

I admit that Genesis 15:17 would make a very unusual life verse. Apart from its context, this verse is nearly impossible to understand. But it is because of the context that I love this verse so. I often tell people that if I were marooned on an island and had only one book, the book I would want with me, of course, would be the Bible. If I could have only one book of the Bible, I would want to have the book of Hebrews because of the way in which it so richly summarizes all the teachings of the Old Testament and relates them to the finished work of Christ in the New

Testament. But if I could have only one verse of the Bible, I would want Genesis 15:17.

GOD SWEARS BY HIMSELF

What is going on here? In Genesis 15, we see God making promises to Abraham. He called to Abraham and said, "Fear not, Abram, I am your shield; your reward shall be very great" (v. 1). Abraham was a little befuddled and asked, "What will you give me, for I continue childless, and the heir of my house is Eliezer of Damascus" (v. 2). Abraham was one of the wealthiest men in the world. He had every material blessing he wanted. However, Eliezer of Damascus, a servant, was Abraham's designated heir because he had no sons. That prompted God to reaffirm an earlier promise by telling Abraham that he would have multitudes of descendents, as many descendants as there are stars in the sky (v. 5). Abraham believed this promise of God, and God counted it to him for righteousness (v. 6). It is this text that the apostle Paul uses in his letter to the Romans to show the Old Testament foundation for the doctrine of justification by faith alone (4:3).

Then God reaffirmed another earlier promise—Abraham

would inherit the land of Canaan (v. 7). But Abraham struggled with the weightiness of this promise. He asked, "O Lord God, how am I to know that I shall possess it?" (v. 8). So God commanded Abraham to get a number of animals, to cut them in two, and to arrange the pieces in two rows, marking out a path (vv. 9–10). It was a bloody mess, a carnage. When Abraham was finished, God put him in a deep sleep and gave to him a vision. That vision is described in verse 17: "When the sun had gone down and it was dark, behold, a smoking fire pot and a flaming torch passed between these pieces."

The fire pot and the flaming torch were theophanies, visible manifestations of the invisible God. Abraham saw a divine manifestation passing between the animal pieces and immediately understood the significance. God was enabling Abraham to know for sure that His promises would come to pass. God said, as it were: "I'm giving you promises, and I cannot swear by anything higher than Myself. I cannot swear by the mountains. I cannot swear by the seas. I cannot swear by the angels. Therefore, I swear to you by Myself. If I fail to keep My promises to you, may I be cut in two like these animals. May I, the immutable God, suffer mutation. May I, the eternal Lord, become temporal. May I, the Infinite, become finite." We know that God was saying these things because the author of the book of Hebrews tells us so: "For when God made a promise to Abraham, since he had no one greater by whom to swear, he swore by himself, saying, 'Surely I will bless you and multiply you'" (6:13–14).

What we see in Genesis 15 is a covenant ceremony that was quite typical for Abraham's time. When two parties made a covenant, they split animals and passed through the pieces, thereby declaring that they deserved to be torn apart should they violate the agreement. In this case, only God passed through the pieces because He alone was making promises. He was instituting His covenant with Abraham.

COVENANTAL SIGNS

What does this event have to do with baptism? When God enters into covenants with His people, making promises of redemption to them, His pattern is to attest to the authenticity of the covenant by giving some kind of external sign. For instance, when He promised Noah that He would never destroy the world again through a flood, God set His bow in the sky. That bow was a visible sign that confirmed the promise of God for the future of this planet. He was saying that every time we see a rainbow, we should be reminded that God has promised never to destroy the world again with a flood.

In a similar manner, after instituting His covenant with Abraham, God gave Abraham and his descendants a sign of their membership in the covenant: circumcision. This sign had a dual significance. On the one hand, the cutting of the foreskin was a sign that God was saying, "I am cutting you out from the rest of fallen humanity and consecrating you as a nation to Myself." At the same time, the sign was a testimony by the people, saying, as it were, "O God, if I fail to keep the terms of this covenant, if I fail to be faithful to You in this covenant relationship, may I be cut off from all of the benefits of Your covenant promises." So circumcision symbolized both the blessings and the curses of God's covenant with Abraham.

The rite of circumcision was given for all generations of Israelites as the sign of the old covenant. That's why, if we were to ask a Jew to identify the sign of God's covenant with His people, he would say that the sign is circumcision.

Just as circumcision was the sign of the old covenant, baptism is the sign of the new covenant. In a very real way, what circumcision was to the Old Testament, baptism is for the New Testament. We see this close connection in Paul's letter to the Colossians. He writes:

> For in him the whole fullness of deity dwells bodily, and you have been filled in him, who is the head of all rule and authority. In him also you were circumcised with a circumcision made without hands, by putting off the body of the flesh, by the circumcision of Christ, having been buried with him in baptism, in which you were also raised with him through faith in the powerful working of God, who raised him from the dead. And you, who were dead in your trespasses and the uncircumcision of your flesh, God made alive together with him, having forgiven us all our trespasses, by canceling the record of debt that stood against us with its legal demands. This he set aside, nailing it to the cross. He disarmed the rulers and authorities and put them to open shame, by triumphing over them in him. (2:9–15)

Paul here tells a body of Gentile believers who have received New Testament baptism that those who are believers have received an internal circumcision. They have a circumcision of the heart, so it is proper and appropriate for them to have the sign of the new covenant, which points beyond itself to all of the benefits of Christ.

COVENANTAL CONTINUITY

Of course, circumcision and baptism are not identical, just as the old covenant and the new covenant are not identical. But these two covenants are not at war. There is no radical antithesis between them. There is an element of discontinuity, which is why we talk about the old and the new. If there were no difference at all between them, the distinction between the old and new covenants would be meaningless. However, the new covenant is not in a state of total discontinuity from the old. In addition to the elements of discontinuity, there are strong elements of continuity. The new covenant does not destroy the old covenant; rather, it fulfills and builds upon it.

Given this continuity, it is to be expected that there are many parallels between the old and new covenants. For example, as we have already seen, both covenants have outward signs of inclusion, circumcision and baptism. Both these signs have to do with the benefits of salvation that God brings to pass in the lives of those who believe. Both circumcision and baptism signify God's promises. And in both cases, it is God who institutes the sign.

God's sovereign act is critically important for understanding the significance of baptism. It means that the integrity of the sign does not rest on the person who administers it or on the person who receives it. If someone is baptized by a minister who later leaves the ministry and abandons the faith, that person does not need to be baptized again. Likewise, the failure of the one who is baptized to lead an exemplary life does not undermine the sign. The integrity of the sign rests upon the person whose promise it is. God's promises stand behind the sign.

That brings us to the central point I want to address in this booklet—the meaning of baptism. We have seen that it is a sign of the new covenant, but what specifically is it a sign of? What is its significance? I once drove from Atlanta to Gainesville, Florida, in a driving rain. I went from city to city—Macon, Tifton, Valdosta, Lake City, Gainesville— so I was eagerly looking for the signs along the road that would tell me the mileage to the next place. At one point, I saw a sign that said, "Valdosta, 74 miles." That was a sign for Valdosta, but that sign was not Valdosta. A sign points beyond itself to something else. In the same way, baptism is not salvation and all that it entails. It is the sign that points us to the benefits of Christ that we receive by faith.

Chapter Four

THE MEANING
OF BAPTISM

Baptism, as we have seen, is a sign. But what does it signify? John's preparatory baptism was a sign of cleansing from sin. He called the people of Israel to take a bath in preparation for the arrival of the Messiah. That significance, of course, is incorporated into New Testament baptism. But New Testament baptism signifies much more than John's baptism indicated. In a sense, because baptism is the sign of the new covenant, it signifies *all* of the benefits that God gives to His people under that covenant, all of the fruits we gain when we embrace the gospel of salvation through Christ alone.

One historic Protestant and Reformed doctrinal statement, the Westminster Confession of Faith, defines baptism this way: "Baptism is a sacrament of the New Testament, ordained by Jesus Christ, not only for the solemn admission of the party baptized into the visible church, but also to be unto him a sign and seal of the covenant of grace, of his engrafting into Christ, of regeneration, of remission of sins, of his giving up unto God, through Jesus Christ, to walk in newness of life: which sacrament is, by Christ's own appointment, to be continued in his church until the end of the world" (28.1).

Perhaps the most outstanding feature of that paragraph is the number of commas, each comma setting off a clause that indicates a particular significance of baptism. Even so, this paragraph is far from exhaustive. That is, baptism signifies even more things than those that are listed in this confessional summary. In this chapter, I want to briefly consider some of the verities that this multifaceted sacrament signifies.

ENGRAFTING INTO CHRIST

The first significance that the confession mentions is "the covenant of grace," which I addressed in the previous chapter. It next speaks of "engrafting into Christ." The term *engrafting* is borrowed from agriculture. Paul uses it when he speaks of the relationship between Gentile believers and Jewish believers, and he describes Gentile believers as wild olive branches that have been grafted into the olive tree, which is the covenant people of God (Rom. 11:17–24). So engrafting portrays something being attached to a host that is alive and growing, in order to draw life from it. Thus, when the confession speaks of engrafting into Christ, it is using one of the most vivid biblical metaphors for what it means to become a Christian.

In the New Testament, there are two Greek words that can be translated into English as "in." One is *eis* and the other is *en*. There is an important distinction between these words that is lost when they are translated into English. *En* means "in" in the sense of "within" or "inside." *Eis* means "in" in the sense of "into." If something is within a circle, it is *en*. If something goes from outside the circle to inside the circle, it is *eis*.

I labor this seemingly minor point because the New Testament teaches us that, in our natural state, we are estranged from God. That means we are outside of fellowship with God, outside of Christ, not in a living communion or fellowship with Him. When people are called to faith in the New Testament, such as when Paul and Silas told the Philippian jailer, "Believe in the Lord Jesus, and you will be saved" (Acts 16:31), the Greek word translated as "in" is *eis*. Thus, Paul and Silas were really saying, "Believe *into* Christ." All who believe *into* Christ are thereafter described by the New Testament as *in* Christ. So when we move from unbelief to faith, we make a transition. We enter into the kingdom of God, into fellowship with God, and into a saving relationship with Jesus Christ after being outside of these things. Salvation, then, is a movement from one realm into another realm, from the kingdom of darkness into the kingdom of light, and the confession captures this idea when it speaks of engrafting *into* Christ.

All who believe into the Lord Jesus Christ enter into a spiritual union with Him, so that we are in Christ and Christ is in us. Because of that, we experience what the Apostles' Creed calls "the communion of saints." This means we have a mystical spiritual union with every single

Christian who has ever lived or ever will live in this world, because we all belong to the same body, Christ. So if I am in Christ and you are in Christ, we share a bond, a spiritual union, not only with Christ but with each other. The New Testament says that we are engrafted into Christ, thereby entering into a mystical union with Him and with His entire body.

Let me hasten to add emphatically that I am not saying that everyone who is baptized is therefore in Christ. I am simply saying that baptism signifies life in Christ. It signifies God's promise to His people of a relationship with Him through His Son by faith. It is the sign of being in Christ rather than in the kingdom of darkness. Like the Old Testament sign of circumcision, baptism is a sign that people are in a special relationship with God, the covenant Lord of His redeemed flock.

Of course, people under the old covenant were, like us, prone to assume that if they had the sign, they automatically had the reality to which the sign pointed. Paul had to rebuke people sharply for assuming that just because they were circumcised they must be in a special relationship with God. Circumcision was the outward sign of the covenant, which signified a redemptive relationship for all of those who were, by faith, connected with God. The same can be said about the New Testament sign.

REGENERATION OF THE HEART

The second major point that the confession points out is our regeneration. Some problems emerge at this point because, as we have seen, one of the great debates that surrounds baptism is whether the sacrament automatically effects regeneration in a recipient. One of the problems in this debate is the fact that the term *regeneration* is used in more than one way in theological discussions. It is used to mean one thing in historic Lutheranism, another thing in historic Roman Catholicism, and another thing in historic Reformed theology.

In classical Reformed theology, the terms *regeneration* or *rebirth* have been used with reference to the supernatural work by which God the Holy Spirit brings to spiritual life a soul that is dead in sin (Eph. 2). Prior to regeneration, we have no inclination for the things of God; we have no desire for Him; we do not want Him in our thinking. But when the Holy Spirit operates on our souls, we cease to be hostile to the things of God and begin to love Christ;

we run to Him and embrace Him because we have been made alive to the things of God. This is the new birth that Jesus describes in John 3. However, others use *regeneration* to indicate not the initial change in the disposition of the soul but the new life in the Christian experience that is wrought after conversion. In other words, *regeneration* is used in Reformed theology to refer to the first step of the new life, which is birth, but others use it as a term for the new life that begins with birth. Those who prefer this use of the term say that rebirth continues as we go through a process of sanctification throughout our lives. It is not a once-for-all, instantaneous, immediate event.

The Reformed view of regeneration is linked to the concept of original sin. Of course, not all churches have the same view of original sin. Virtually every church in the World Council of Churches would confess that man is fallen, that every person is born in a state of corruption inherited from Adam and Eve. But huge debates ensue about the degree of that corruption. Some groups, such as Pelagians, Socinians, and some modern liberals, deny that there is any inherited corruption. But within orthodox Christianity, there is agreement that something happened to the constituent nature of humanity in the fall of Adam, leaving us either severely weakened in terms of our moral strength or, as Reformed theology teaches, morally unable to incline ourselves to the things of God.

This state of corruption is called original sin. We are not sinners because we sin; we sin because we are sinners. The corrupt fruit flows out of our corrupt natures. When we sin, we are doing what comes naturally to us as fallen creatures.

This sinfulness is seen in metaphorical ways in Scripture. It is portrayed in terms of spiritual impurity or uncleanness. For instance, the furniture of the tabernacle and the temple in the Old Testament included a special vessel called the laver. This object symbolized the necessity of a cleansing rite to renew a person from his state of moral impurity.

What does this teaching mean for baptism? Baptism is a sign of God's promise to regenerate His people, to liberate them from the moral bondage of original sin, to cleanse their souls from guilt and purify them so they can enter into a saving relationship with Him. So all of what happens in the Holy Spirit's work of changing us from the inside out is signified by the sacrament of baptism. That's why the use of water is at the heart of baptism. It is a sign of cleansing from sin, which is regeneration to new life in Christ.

REMISSION AND SURRENDER

The third significance that the confession identifies is "remission of sins." In other words, it is the sign of one of the consequences of our faith in Christ, which is justification. When God justifies us, He declares us just by the remission of sins. Our justification is rooted and grounded in the ministry of Christ, who took our sins upon Himself and satisfied the demands of God's justice through His atoning work. On the one hand, Jesus' death on the cross satisfied the justice of the Father. On the other hand, like the Old Testament scapegoat, to which the sins of the people were ceremonially transferred and which was then sent away into the darkness outside the camp (Lev. 16), Christ became our sin-bearer, our scapegoat, who removed our sins from us to the uttermost. So when baptism is administered, the promise of God to remit our sins and to remove them from us as far as the east is from the west (Ps. 103:12) is signified.

Finally, the confession points to our "giving up unto God, through Jesus Christ, to walk in newness of life." Here the confession touches on our surrender to God, our turning from our own willful ways to follow Christ in submission to His lordship. Having been "crucified with Christ" (Gal. 2:20) in our mystical union with Him, we are raised to new life, with new hearts that are able to choose God's ways. We want to walk in those ways, and baptism is a sign of this surrender and the resulting change.

It is important to note that the confession concludes by saying that baptism is, "by Christ's own appointment, to be continued in his church until the end of the world." Wherever and whenever the gospel makes inroads, new believers are to be baptized. Anyone who suggests that baptism is unnecessary is in defiance of Christ's own commandment.

THE BAPTISM OF THE SPIRIT

Moving beyond the points mentioned in the Westminster Confession, I would like to single out two more. First, New Testament baptism in water points to the Christian's baptism by the Holy Spirit.

Throughout the twentieth century, a major movement in the church placed great emphasis on the concept of the baptism of the Holy Spirit. Charismatic and Pentecostal believers stressed the Spirit's baptism as a second experience of grace. This was a departure from classical Christian thought, which understands the baptism of the Holy Spirit to refer to the equipping of all believers with a measure of power for ministry.

What, then, is the baptism of the Spirit and how does it relate to water baptism? In the Old Testament, a few individuals had the *charismata*, charismatic gifts of grace that enabled them to perform significant tasks. The Holy Spirit came upon David to enable him to carry out his role as king (1 Sam. 16:13). He came upon the prophets, anointing them and enabling them to be agents of revelation (2 Chron. 15:1; 20:14). In the period of the judges, when unique gifts were needed for leadership, the Lord raised up men and gifted them to deliver His people (Judg. 2:16; 13:25).

The person in the Old Testament who manifested perhaps the most intense degree of this baptism and empowering by the Holy Spirit for ministry was Moses, whom God endowed with extraordinary gifts of leadership to be the mediator of the old covenant. On one occasion, when the people were unhappy that they had nothing except manna to eat, Moses began to despair and asked God to kill him because the burden of satisfying the people was too great for him (Num. 11:15). God commanded

Moses to gather seventy elders of Israel and declared that He would "take some of the Spirit that is on you and put it on them, and they shall bear the burden of the people with you, so that you may not bear it yourself alone" (v. 17). Moses did as he was instructed, and God took some of the Spirit's endowment that was upon Moses and anointed these seventy elders to help him.

In a rather strange addendum to this story, we learn that two of the designated seventy elders did not gather with the others at the tabernacle but remained in the camp. Nevertheless, God endowed them with His Spirit, and they began to prophesy in the camp, just as the other elders were prophesying at the tabernacle. When Joshua heard about it, he was upset and urged Moses to tell the two men to desist. But Moses said: "Are you jealous for my sake? Would that all of the LORD's people were prophets, that the LORD would put his Spirit on them!" (v. 29).

That wish of Moses became part of the content of prophecy later when the prophet Joel announced: "It shall come to pass afterward, that I will pour out my Spirit on all flesh; your sons and daughters shall prophesy, your old men shall dream dreams, and your young men shall see visions. Even on the male and female servants in those days

I will pour out my Spirit" (Joel 2:28–29). When the day of Pentecost came in the New Testament, all of the Jewish believers who were present received the baptism of the Holy Spirit (Acts 2:2–4). When that happened, the apostle Peter said, "This is what was uttered through the prophet Joel: 'And in the last days it shall be, God declares, that I will pour out my Spirit on all flesh'" (vv. 16–17a). So the New Testament saw the Pentecost experience as the fulfillment of Joel's prophecy.

As the gospel began to spread, there were outpourings of the Spirit among the Samaritans (Acts 8:14–17), the God-fearers (10:44), and the Gentiles (19:1–6). The apostles witnessed these events and concluded that since God had given His Spirit to each group, there were no second-class citizens in the new covenant, no limitations on Samaritans, Greeks, or other Gentile converts. Based on this truth, Paul affirmed, "To each is given the manifestation of the Spirit for the common good" (1 Cor. 12:7).

So, according to classical Christianity, the idea of the baptism of the Holy Spirit is this: Every Christian receives not only the Spirit's work of regeneration, but also the Spirit's empowering for participation in the ministry of the gospel. That does not mean everyone is called to be a pastor, a preacher, or an evangelist, but every Christian has been set apart and empowered by the Holy Spirit, like those seventy elders of Israel. But whereas only some believers in the Old Testament received the empowerment of the baptism of the Holy Spirit, every believer in the New Testament receives it.

Thus, even though there is a distinction between water baptism and Spirit baptism, one of the things the new covenant sign of baptism indicates is the participation of every believer in the power and anointing of the Holy Spirit. Water baptism is a sign of Spirit baptism.

DEATH AND RESURRECTION

Finally, New Testament baptism is a sign of our death and resurrection with Christ. Baptism indicates our identification with the death of Christ; by it, we confess our faith that His death was for us, that in His atonement He paid the penalty for our sin. He was not raised from the dead simply for His own vindication, but as the New Testament teaches us, He was raised as the firstborn of many brethren (Rom. 8:29). So, the conquest of death, on behalf of all who are in Christ, is also signified by baptism.

As you can see, baptism is full of rich symbolism that points to all the things God does for us when He delivers us from our sin. The promises of God to His beloved people through Jesus Christ are on brilliant display when the sacrament of baptism is administered. These things were not part of the significance of the preparatory baptism of John the Baptist. New Testament baptism communicates all that Christ Jesus accomplished for us.

It is important to note that Paul speaks of circumcision as both a sign and a seal (Rom. 4:11), so Protestants historically have used the same language for baptism. The concept of sealing is one of the most neglected teachings of the New Testament. It tells us, for example, that everyone who is in Christ is not only reborn of the Holy Spirit and empowered for ministry, but sealed by the Spirit. Each believer receives the "earnest" of the Spirit. When a person buys a house, he is asked to put down earnest money, which constitutes his promise to pay the balance. Some people default on their promises, showing that they were not really in earnest when they put down their money. But when God makes a down payment and promises to finish the transaction, we need not worry about Him making the full payment. With this language, the New Testament is teaching that everyone who is born again and receives the Holy Spirit has God's promise that He will do the rest. We are sealed for full salvation.

In the ancient world, the seal was the symbol of ownership, of authenticity, and of authority. When a king sent out an edict or an official communication of some kind, the document was sealed with a drop of hot wax, and then the king pressed his signet ring into the wax, giving it his mark or brand to prove its authenticity. In the same way, the gift of the Spirit seals the believer, for God gives His Spirit only to those who are His. The Spirit is God's brand upon the sheep of His flock. Thus, the incredible promise of God of salvation to all who believe is conveyed by the God who never goes back on His word.

Chapter Five

THE MODE
OF BAPTISM

W hat is the proper way for a person to be baptized? Is there a specific mode of baptism that is essential to the authenticity of the sacrament? Of all the debates that have attended the sacrament of baptism, the question of the proper mode has become and remained one of the most persistent and divisive.

Various churches in Christian history have answered

this question by asserting that one method or another is the only valid method. In recent decades, some scholars and theologians have argued strenuously that the New Testament method of baptism is immersion, and some have gone so far as to insist that if a person is not baptized by immersion, he is not genuinely baptized. Others have countered that assertion by declaring that immersion is not even a legitimate form of baptism. Of course, each of the other modes—sprinkling, pouring, and dipping—has vociferous proponents and critics, too.

As I said earlier, I do not think these kinds of debates are carried on by people who like to argue simply for the sake of argument. I believe these differences arise because sincere Christians have a genuine and deep desire to do what is pleasing to God, so they want to perform the sacrament biblically. If a person believes that Scripture commands that baptism be performed by immersion, he might legitimately come to the conclusion that unless immersion is practiced, something less than baptism takes place.

The question, of course, is whether Scripture actually *commands* one specific mode of baptism. This is not an easy question to answer.

EVIDENCE FROM THE GREEK TEXT

In the New Testament, the Greek word that is translated as "baptize" is *baptizo*. This word usually means "to immerse, sink, drown, or go under," and it is for this reason that proponents of immersion argue that theirs is the proper mode for baptism.

In some of the New Testament passages where *baptizo* appears, the context appears to bolster the argument that immersion is the proper mode for baptism. For instance, many conclusions are drawn from John's baptism because it took place at the Jordan River and indeed John baptized (*baptizo*) "in the river" (Matt. 3:6). It is assumed that John must have required people to go into the river so that they could be immersed. However, Scripture never says that people were immersed when they went down into the river, merely that they were baptized there. Also, we have ancient Christian art that depicts people being baptized in a river, but they are standing almost waist-deep in the water and the one who is doing the baptizing is scooping up water from the river and pouring it on the heads of the recipients. It appears the recipients went into the water not to be immersed but so that it would be a simple matter to pour water over their heads.

Another New Testament narrative that is cited to support immersion is Philip's baptism of the Ethiopian eunuch, recorded in Acts 8. Luke writes that Philip and the eunuch "went down into the water" (Acts 8:38), and there Philip baptized (*baptizo*) the man. Again, however, the text does not specifically say that the eunuch was immersed. It does say that "they came up out of the water" (v. 39), but clearly this phrase does not mean that both Philip and the eunuch went under the water before coming up again. It simply means that they climbed the bank of the river, just as they had descended it. Here again, the mode of the baptism is not specifically revealed.

The issue becomes more complex when we see that *baptizo* sometimes is used when the context clearly does not suggest immersion. In Mark 7, we are told that the Pharisees noticed some of Jesus' disciples eating food without first washing their hands. The washing in view was a ceremonial cleansing that was prescribed not by God's law but by the Jewish rabbinical traditions that had arisen. By way of background, Mark notes that the Pharisees would not eat unless they had washed in this ceremonial way, especially after coming from the marketplace (vv. 3b–4). It is interesting that the word translated as "wash" in verse 4 is *baptizo*, and it clearly does not imply full-body immersion. Likewise, in Luke 11:38, we read of a Pharisee who was astonished that Jesus did not "wash" before dinner. Again, the word *baptizo* is used here, and again it clearly does not mean total immersion in water. Sometimes *baptizo* is used in classical Greek simply to mean "to bathe or wash," and we see examples of that usage in these passages.

THE "DIPPING" OF NAAMAN

Another biblical story that seems to argue for immersion is found in 2 Kings 5. Interestingly, the word *baptizo* also appears in this story in the Septuagint, the Greek version of the Hebrew Scriptures. The name of this work comes from the Latin phrase *Interpretatio septuaginta virorum*, which literally means "interpretation of the seventy men," because this translation was produced in antiquity by a team of seventy Jewish scholars. The translation work was done during the period of the Hellenization of the ancient world, when Alexander the Great was building his empire and beginning his program of introducing Greek culture throughout the

Mediterranean region. Greek was becoming the common language, so generations of Jewish people were growing up speaking and reading Greek rather than Hebrew. The Hebrew Scriptures were translated into the Greek language so that Greek-speaking Jews might read them. In seeking to determine the precise meaning of Greek terms in the New Testament, scholars examine the Septuagint, paying close attention to which Greek words were used to translate Hebrew ideas from the Old Testament.

In 2 Kings 5, we find the story of Naaman, the commander of the army of the king of Syria. Naaman, who was afflicted with leprosy, was advised to go to Israel to seek healing from the prophet Elisha. When Naaman came to Elisha's home, the prophet sent a servant out to tell him to "wash" seven times in the Jordan River (v. 10). The Hebrew word translated as "wash" here, *rachats*, carries the meaning of "bathe or wash," just as *baptizo* sometimes does. It appears again in verses 12 and 13 as Naaman debated whether to follow the prophet's instructions. But when Naaman finally went to the Jordan, he "dipped himself" seven times (v. 14). The English term used here is different because the Hebrew term is different; it is the word *tabal*, which means "to dip or plunge." However, in the Septuagint, the word translated as "dipped" is *baptizo*.

At first glance, this use of *baptizo* seems to strengthen the argument that it meant immersion. It seems Naaman did something more than "wash" himself; he dipped or plunged himself under the Jordan's water. The difficulty is that the Septuagint usually translates *tabal* with a different Greek word, *bapto*, which means simply "to dip." We see examples of this in Leviticus 4:17, where the priest was commanded to "dip his finger in the blood and sprinkle it seven times before the LORD in front of the veil"; in Leviticus 14:6, where the priest was instructed to "take the live bird with the cedarwood and the scarlet yarn and the hyssop, and dip them and the live bird in the blood of the bird that was killed over the fresh water"; in Joshua 3:15, which says, "the feet of the priests bearing the ark were dipped in the brink of the water"; in Ruth 2:14, where Boaz tells Ruth to "Come here and eat some bread and dip your morsel in the wine"; and in 1 Samuel 14:27, where we are told that Jonathan "put out the tip of the staff that was in his hand and dipped it in the honeycomb." In all of these instances, the Hebrew word *tabal* is translated by the Greek word *bapto* in the Septuagint.

As you can see, *tabal* carries a wide range of meanings in these passages. In some cases, the object being dipped seems to be wholly immersed, but in others it clearly is not. In some cases, the dipping occurs in the context of a formal ceremony in the tabernacle, while in other cases it involves a meal. These passages, then, provide little help in understanding what "dipping" means in 2 Kings 5:14.

That leaves us with the question of why the seventy elders used *baptizo* rather than *bapto* to translate *tabal* in 2 Kings 5:14. I do not believe we can know for certain, but I personally think it had to do with the fact that leprosy represented ceremonial uncleanness, and Naaman was told to perform a ritual that would remove his impurity. Just as the Pharisees would "wash" (*baptizo*) their hands so as to be ceremonially clean before eating, Naaman was told to "wash" so that he would be ceremonially clean, and he responded by "dipping" himself in the Jordan (*baptizo*).

So in the end, I'm not sure we can make a conclusive case from Scripture that one mode of baptism is to be preferred over another.

FLEXIBILITY IN THE EARLY CHURCH

I believe the early church recognized this lack of certainty in Scripture. In a place where water was scarce and where few congregations had their own buildings, much less baptismal fonts or pools, the church was not extremely particular about how baptism was accomplished. We see this from the *Didache*, a church "manual" dating from the late first century or early second century:

> But concerning baptism, thus shall ye baptize Having first recited all these things, baptize in the name of the Father and of the Son and of the Holy Spirit in living (running) water. But if thou hast not living water, then baptize in other water; and if thou art not able in cold, then in warm. But if thou hast neither, then pour water on the head thrice in the name of the Father and of the Son and of the Holy Spirit. But before the baptism let him that baptizeth and him that is baptized fast, and any others also who are able; and thou shalt order him that is baptized to fast a day or two before. (Chapter 7, translation by J. B. Lightfoot)

The writer of the *Didache* was dogmatic about the use of the Trinitarian formula in baptism, but was flexible as to the mode that was employed. So, from the earliest days,

Christians used a variety of modes to baptize. The mode did not greatly matter, so long as the sign character of the sacrament as a cleansing was communicated.

My conclusion is that the question of the mode of baptism should not divide Christians. The issue has been examined and debated for two thousand years, but full agreement is no closer. This is an area of church practice where we are called to forbear with one another and not cast aspersions against those who practice a mode different from the one we prefer. The bottom line is that everyone is trying to say basically the same thing through whatever mode is employed—that the recipient is included in the body of Christ and that he or she has been cleansed from sin. The mode that we use should not be a cause of divisions in the church.

Chapter Six

THE CASE FOR INFANT BAPTISM

I t has been my experience that when I address the subject of infant baptism, I get a sudden increase in the volume of my mail, and most of it is not very complimentary. The reason, of course, is that in the evangelical church today, the majority report is in favor of what is called believer's baptism.

This preference has not always held sway. Throughout church history, the practice of infant baptism has been far and away the majority report. Even today, there are far more denominations that practice infant baptism than do not, but those denominations tend to be smaller, so the membership in denominations that do not practice infant baptism far outnumbers that of denominations that do. Thus, a person who believes in and practices infant baptism must acknowledge that, in terms of the contemporary evangelical scene, he is in the minority.

Of course, it's a very dangerous thing to try to discern what is the good and proper way to please God simply by counting noses. Just because a position at a particular time is favored by a majority of denominations or believers does not establish its legitimacy. Still, historical precedents should give someone pause before he becomes too dogmatic about the impropriety of the baptism of infants. Since infant baptism has been the majority view throughout church history, I think that the judgment of charity requires every believer to at least ask why so many have been favorable to that position, even if he is convinced that the view of the majority is incorrect, That doesn't mean abandoning one's opposition to infant baptism; it simply means taking time to investigate why so many others see things differently.

When I began teaching in a seminary, the student body was made up chiefly of three denominational groups: Presbyterians, Episcopalians, and Baptists. Both the Presbyterians and the Episcopalians practiced infant baptism, but the Baptists did not. I was charged with teaching Systematic Theology III, which covered the doctrine of the church and the sacraments. I was concerned about teaching on the sacraments because of the split among my students and because I was a Presbyterian professor who believed in infant baptism. I asked myself, "What if I persuade these Baptist students of the legitimacy of infant baptism when they're so close to being ordained in a community that does not believe in it?" Finally, I devised what seemed to be a fair way to deal with the subject: I assigned the Presbyterians and Episcopalians a ten-page paper on the case for believer's baptism, and I assigned the Baptists a ten-page paper on the case for infant baptism. By this method, I believed that all the students would come to know what the proponents of the opposite position were saying. Afterward, a number of those students expressed how helpful it was to them to study what their opponents believed.

The New Testament nowhere explicitly commands Christians to baptize their infant children. This represents a change from the Old Testament, where there was an explicit mandate for parents to circumcise male babies. But by the same token, there is no explicit prohibition in the New Testament against the baptism of infants. The New Testament does not give explicit instructions in either direction, so the case for or against infant baptism must be made on inferences and implications drawn from the text of Scripture. This factor, more than any other, should cause us to be very careful in our interactions with those who disagree with us on this matter.

Let me work through some of the implications and inferences that have made infant baptism the majority report in church history.

INFERENCES FROM SCRIPTURE

First, there is the link in Scripture between the Old Testament sign of the covenant, circumcision, and the New Testament sign of the covenant, baptism. As we have already seen, circumcision and baptism are not identical, but they do have very important aspects in common, not the least of which is that both are signs of the covenant. We know beyond any dispute that the old covenant sign was given to adults after they made professions of faith and to infants before they were capable of making professions of faith. For example, Abraham believed as an adult and then received the sign of the covenant, but his son Isaac received the sign of the covenant before he believed.

That is very important, because the most common argument against infant baptism is that it signifies things that flow from faith, and since infants are not capable of expressing or embracing faith, they should not receive the sign. But if that argument were correct, it would nullify the legitimacy of circumcision in the Old Testament. If we reject infant baptism on the basis of the principle that a sign that involves faith must never be given until after faith is present, we also negate the legitimacy of circumcision in the Old Testament.

Second, the New Testament clearly sees the new covenant as better than the old covenant (Heb. 7:22; 8:6), partly because it is more inclusive rather than less inclusive. Since infants received the sign of the old covenant, were they not given the sign of the new covenant, that would mean that the new covenant is less inclusive than the old covenant.

Third, there is a similar practice in regard to the covenant signs and households under both covenants.

One argument that is used strenuously against infant baptism is that there is no record of infants being baptized in the New Testament. Every time we read of someone being baptized, it is an adult. Thus, some infer that only adults should be baptized.

I acknowledge that the argument is technically correct—we do not see a single specific reference to an infant child being baptized in the scriptural records about the early church. However, there are about twelve accounts of baptisms in the Bible, and three of those accounts report the baptism not only of a particular adult but of his or her household, which may have included infants. Some New Testament scholars, such as Oscar Cullman of Switzerland, argue that the Greek word *oikos*, which is translated as "household" in the New Testament, not only may include infant children but has specific reference to infants.

In any case, we see households being given the sign of the covenant in the New Testament, and we see the same principle at work in the Old Testament, when Abraham, for instance, was circumcised along with all the men of his household (Gen. 17:26–27). Since that concept of household inclusion carried over into the New Testament, and since we know that households receiving the covenant sign in the Old Testament frequently included infants, the three examples of household baptism in the New Testament certainly argue for the propriety of infant baptism.

CHILDREN SET APART AS HOLY

Fourth, we must consider the language of 1 Corinthians 7, where Paul gives instructions about marriage and divorce. He writes:

> To the rest I say (I, not the Lord) that if any brother has a wife who is an unbeliever, and she consents to live with him, he should not divorce her. If any woman has a husband who is an unbeliever, and he consents to live with her, she should not divorce him. For the unbelieving husband is made holy because of his wife, and the unbelieving wife is made holy because of her husband. Otherwise your children would be unclean, but as it is, they are holy. (vv. 12–14)

How can we understand Paul's strange assertions that a husband can be made holy because of his wife, that a wife can be made holy because of her husband, and that their children can somehow be made holy in this context? We tend to think of sanctification as that process by which the Holy Spirit brings us into conformity to Christ after our justification. Some people read this text with that idea in mind, saying, "Well, if I'm a believer but my wife isn't, and if she's sanctified by virtue of being married to me, then she must also be justified." If that were true, there would be more than one way to be saved—you could be justified by your own faith or by marrying someone who has faith. But that is against the clear teaching of the New Testament. So the apostle's teaching about sanctification here obviously does not refer to that process by which we are brought into conformity to Christ after our justification.

What, then, does this text mean? To get at the answer, let us try to determine how a first-century Jewish person would have understood these words. Remember that the primary biblical meaning of the verb *sanctify* is "to consecrate, to set apart." In fact, to be sanctified in the Old Testament was to be purified or set apart by some ritual of purification, and the primary such ritual was circumcision. So Paul is saying, using language that is filled to the brim with covenant import, that an unbelieving husband is *set apart* by his believing wife and an unbelieving wife is *set apart* by her believing husband. Why? So that their children will not be unclean. In the old covenant, being unclean meant being outside the camp, separated and apart from the covenant community of God. Paul's words here, then, mean that by virtue of the faith of only one parent, children are holy. This is an explicit New Testament affirmation that the infant child of one believer in a marriage is in a state of consecration. The child is not considered unclean, but is set apart and considered holy. And the rite that consecrates the child in the new covenant community is baptism.

THE TESTIMONY OF HISTORY

Finally, there is the testimony of church history in support of infant baptism. It has been argued that not only is infant baptism not mentioned in the pages of Scripture, it is not explicitly mentioned in any documents from the early church. This claim is true. The literature from the late first century and even into the early second century does not mention the baptism of children. The first reference to infant baptism is from around the year 150, more than one hundred years after the beginning of the apostolic community. So the argument is put forward that a ritual was devised in the second century that represented a departure from the pristine practice of the early church.

The problem with this argument is that the reference from around the year 150 indicates that infant baptism was the universal practice of the Christian church. Arguments from silence are dangerous, but it would be a strange and astonishing thing if there had been a significant departure from the purity of the apostolic community that infected the entire Christian world by the middle of the second century without a word of concern or protest being raised. In other words, the fact that the practice of infant baptism seems to have spread to the whole Christian community within a hundred years with no known protest is a further indication that the acceptability of giving infant children the covenant sign was simply assumed by the early church. It seems that infant baptism was administered because it represented a continuation of the practice that had more than two thousand years of precedent in the house of Israel.

These, then, I judge, are some valid and compelling reasons for the practice of infant baptism. Here again, however, I urge that those who believe in infant baptism and those who support believer's baptism will practice the judgment of charity and not let their diverging views become a source of division.

About the Author

Dr. R. C. Sproul is the founder and chairman of Ligonier Ministries, an international multimedia ministry based in Sanford, Florida. He also serves as senior minister of preaching and teaching at Saint Andrew's, a Reformed congregation in Sanford, and as president of Reformation Bible College, and his teaching can be heard around the world on the daily radio program *Renewing Your Mind*.

During his distinguished academic career, Dr. Sproul helped train men for the ministry as a professor at several theological seminaries.

He is the author of more than eighty books, including *The Holiness of God, Chosen by God, The Invisible Hand, Faith Alone, A Taste of Heaven, Truths We Confess, The Truth of the Cross*, and *The Prayer of the Lord*. He also served as general editor of *The Reformation Study Bible* and has written several children's books, including *The Prince's Poison Cup*.

Dr. Sproul and his wife, Vesta, make their home in Longwood, Florida.